Not Just Another Move

By Andrea Kushka
Illlustrated by Jason Wolff

Diana took a deep breath. She was very upset but wanted her voice to be steady when she spoke.

"When do we have to leave?" she asked.

"As soon as the house is sold," her father replied.

"And the spaceship is ready," her mother added.

Her brother, Leo, kept eating his breakfast. He didn't mind another move but then he was only a small child. It was different for Diana.

Mrs. Fuller was an inventor whose head was full of creative ideas. She had invented ways to use wool as fuel, make bread from mold, and control bad weather.

Mr. Fuller was an engineer who made Mrs. Fuller's wild plans into reality. He created the machines that did the actual work.

Now their inventions would be used on Mars. Mr. and Mrs. Fuller were very excited.

Mr. and Mrs. Fuller were already happily making lists. Their pleasure made Diana bold.

She shouted, "You can't make me move again. I won't do it!"

They stopped and looked at her as if she were a two-headed creature.

"That is a childish remark," her mother said mildly.

"There will be time for good-byes," her father said kindly.

Diana ran blindly to her room.

The Mars colony was not that old. The first colonists had arrived ten years ago. Today about 5,000 men, women, and children were spread among the three settlements. They lived under gigantic plastic domes. These protected them from Mars's cruel climate and deadly air. When they left the domes, they wore spacesuits with gold-tinted helmets and dual air tanks. The people looked sort of odd but no one seemed to mind.

Diana read all this and more on her hover computer. Mars sounded dreadful.

Mrs. Fuller knocked softly and then entered Diana's room.

"I know you want to stay here instead of going to Mars, but we would miss you too much," she said. "This will be a real adventure. Just like the ones in your favorite video books. You may like it."

Diana hadn't thought of the move like that.

"It will be only for a year or two at most. Think of all the good stories you'll have when you get back to Earth. After all, not many people have gone to Mars."

That *was* a pleasant thought. Diana could see herself holding people spellbound with her incredible tales.

"Maybe moving to Mars wouldn't be too bad," Diana thought.

Leo marched into the room.

"What are you guys doing in here?" he demanded boldly.

His arrival ended Diana's daydream. She sighed. She still dreaded the move, but her heart didn't feel quite as cold and heavy.

"Let's find those lists. We have a lot to do if we are moving soon," she told her mother.

Mrs. Fuller put her arm around Diana's shoulders as they left the room.